R U THE UGLY GIRL?

If You Teach Self-Worth through the Eyes of Christ
Jesus, Self-Esteem Will Come with Humility

TAKIA TEKE

Illustrated by

J. Sterling Jackson

WESTBOW
PRESS®
A DIVISION OF THOMAS NELSON
& ZONDERVAN

WestBow Press books may be ordered through booksellers or by contacting:

WestBow Press
A Division of Thomas Nelson & Zondervan
1663 Liberty Drive
Bloomington, IN 47403
www.westbowpress.com
1 (866) 928-1240

ISBN: 978-1-5127-6680-6 (sc)
ISBN: 978-1-5127-6681-3 (e)

Library of Congress Control Number: 2016919932

Print information available on the last page.

WestBow Press rev. date: 2/1/2017

ACKNOWLEDGMENTS

Special thanks to everyone who believed in me. I know that God placed a love for writing in my heart and mind as he did my mother Carol's and grandmother Ruth's. They both encouraged me to follow my dreams and to love the lord with all my heart. ("A man's heart plans his way but the Lord directs his steps." Proverbs 16:9) Publishing my first book and being able to share it with my friends and family truly means the world to me. When we put God first, he gives us his best.

I want to thank my aunt Laketa Ezell, who has gone on to be with the Lord. She was the first to tell me that I was a writer. To my aunt Sandra Winston, I miss you. Special thanks to Debbie, Jeanette, Corey, Korey, Chyna, Cameryn, Carrinton, Darius, Weldon, Lashonda, C.C., Verdell, LaQuetia, Brittnie, Johnathan, Pastor and First Lady Marchbanks, everyone at Stretched Out Arms Church, Mary, all my aunts, uncles, cousins, friends and most especially Shawn, Talmage, Judah, Jael, Kam, Xoe, Kellan, Shawn Jr.. SEIU, thank you! #onefleshministry

"For God so loved the world that he gave his only begotten son Christ Jesus"

(John 3:16).

Last Day of School!

Today was the best day of my life, and it started like all the others. God woke me up.

I brushed my teeth and thanked the Lord for another day.

This was the last day of school, the end-of-the-year carnival. It seemed this day would never come. I was so excited.

Since today was super special, only my best dress would do—and let's not forget the shoes. When I looked in the mirror, I saw I was perfect! Oh, I almost forgot my headband.

Today, I say good-bye to Grace Jr. High and hello to Wisdom High School!

Carnival, carnival, carnival!

Ferris wheels,

funnel cakes, and ...

friends!

When I first arrived at school, there was a girl sitting on the steps next to the flagpole.

She was crying. She had her hands folded across her lap, and her head was down.

The strangest thing was that I was the only one who noticed her. Every other person—teacher, student, and parent—walked right past her. Even Mr. Gab did, and he noticed everyone. Yes, everybody.

"Excuse me. My name is Faith. Are you all right?" I asked the girl.

She mumbled, "No. A tall girl called my clothes ugly and said my shirt and tights didn't match. I searched my entire closet, and my mom helped me pick them out. Do you think my clothes are ugly?" She anxiously awaited my answer.

I looked at her clothes and then her shoes. I thought, *I'd never wear that.* And at that very moment, I heard a whisper.

"**Don't be the ugly girl.** *Ugly girls say mean things. We're all unique in God's eyes, even in style.*"

I looked at her, smiled, and said, "I like what you're wearing because you like it. This would be a boring world if we all dressed alike, and clothes can only make the outside beautiful. When you say mean things, you look ugly on the inside and the outside. That's why God looks at the heart."

She laughed. Her laugh made me feel good inside. As we got to our feet, the bell rang, and Mr. Gab called to me, "Faith, come now. You don't want to be late."

I turned my head for a *sminute*—that's half of a minute—and the girl was gone. I thought, I hope she has a wonderful last day of school.

As I walked down the hall, humming my happy song, I noticed everyone I passed was in a wonderful mood. But when I entered my classroom, everyone was laughing at the meanest girl in school.

She bent down to pick up her pencil and split her shorts right down the middle. I wanted to laugh with the class, and maybe she deserved it. *She called me "four eyes" over a thousand times. She'd even hidden my glasses. When Mr. Gab found them under his hat on his desk, the lenses were missing.*

To make things worse, she told me she did it.

And just as I was about to laugh, I heard a whisper.

"Don't be the ugly girl. *Ugly girls laugh when someone is hurting. What if you were in her shoes? What if she were you? She needs a friend."*

I then remembered she was nice to everyone until that cold day in November when she couldn't find her coat …

5

... and had to ride the bus home in the cold.

I guess sometimes pain can make you mean, but kindness always helps you find friends. I gave her my sweater to wrap around her waist and said, "Sorry you tore your shorts."

She asked, "Why are you being nice to me?"

"That's what friends do," I responded. "It's never too late to make a friend!"

I noticed Mr. Gab watching and smiling. It felt good to do something nice. But when she asked, "Faith, can we be friends forever?" I felt *super* good inside. Like Mr. Gab always says, "A friend must first show herself friendly."

As I sat, anxiously awaiting the bell, I could see the Ferris wheel going around and around from the window. I wanted to be the first to ride everything.

As Mr. Gab passed out the white envelopes with our names on them, which were filled with our carnival tickets, it felt like time was moving oh so slowly.

Was this a moment when patience was needed? Was this a moment when good things came to those who waited? That's what my mother always said. But it couldn't be; I wasn't the only one excited.

When Mr. Gab passed the last envelope to the girl in the front row, I wondered, Where is mine?

"Faith," Mr. Gab asked, "are you sure you purchased tickets?"

"Yes. Remember, we laughed when I was the first in line and it wasn't time? We were only going to math class."

"You're right," Mr. Gab responded. "I do remember. Okay, class, please make sure you have the right envelope. Faith's is missing. Check and see if there are two stuck together."

I felt a little sad, so I raised my hand to go to the restroom. As I walked down the hall, I said a prayer.

"Dear Lord, it's Faith again. I need a moment of your time. I believe you can hear me and you see all things. I know you know where my envelope is. Can you please show me? Thank you, in Jesus's name. I do believe!"

As I walked backed to class, I saw a girl in a yellow shirt, standing by my classroom. She was holding an envelope, and it had my name on it.

My carnival tickets!

I screamed, using my inside voice. When the girl wearing the yellow shirt lifted her head and saw my enormous smile, she didn't smile back. I couldn't believe what she did next. She placed my envelope behind her back and then walked to Mr. Mike's class.

I knew the right thing to do was to tell my teacher, but at that moment, *I was angry. Yes, I was very upset! I followed her, thinking, I should snatch my envelope right out of her hand. It's mine!*

Then at that moment, I heard a whisper.

"**Don't be the ugly girl.** *Ugly girls take things that don't belong to them. Ugly girls steal. The truth always shines through when you do what's right.*"

I thought, Whether it is or isn't my envelope, the right thing to do is to tell my teacher. But what if I'm wrong and it's not my envelope?

Mr. Mike, Mr. Gab, the girl in the yellow shirt, and I met in the hallway outside of Mr. Mike's class.

The girl in the yellow shirt apologized as she gave me my envelope. "I'm sorry, Faith. I took your carnival tickets. My parents didn't have the money to buy me any, but I know that's not a good reason to take what doesn't belong to me. Please forgive me."

As I looked into her sad eyes, I thought, Everyone has to ask for forgiveness once or twice in life. I know it's not right to take things that are not ours, but if God can forgive me when I'm wrong or mean to someone, I can forgive her.

I responded, "I forgive you, and if it's okay with Mr. Gab and Mr. Mike, I'd like to share my tickets with you. I have more than enough."

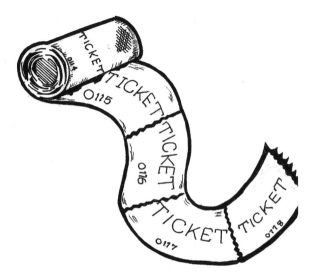

The girl in the yellow shirt smiled as our teachers both replied, "Sure, that's fine."

I felt good inside!

As we entered the classroom, the bell rang, and all the children started screaming, "It's noon! It's carnival time!" As we lined up one last time, two students started pushing, shoving, and yelling at each other.

"I was here first!"

"No, I was!"

"Move!"

"I'm going to tell!"

Mr. Gab shouted, "Enough! You both go to the back of the line."

As both girls sadly walked past me, one girl with long black hair gave me the meanest look and asked, "What are you looking at?"

And then she called me a bad name.

Mr. Gab didn't hear her, and I couldn't believe she had said it. I knew words didn't hurt, *but I wanted to call her a name just as mean as what she had called me.* But at that moment, I heard a whisper.

"Don't be the ugly girl. *Ugly girls say bad words. Beautiful words make God smile. Love and kindness can make all girls beautiful. God hears us, even our whispers."*

So I said to the girl with the long black hair, "I'm sorry you're angry, but I didn't do it and I didn't deserve to be called a bad name. No one does. So I think you owe me an apology. If you wouldn't say that word in front of your parents, don't say it in front of God or to me. God hears and sees everything, right and wrong."

She said, "I'm sorry. You're right. My mom would be extremely mad if she heard me say that word to you. I'm sorry!"

"If God can forgive me, I can forgive you," I responded. "We're too pretty to say bad words. We should never speak to each other by cursing. Bad words make us look ugly. And who wants to be ugly like a witch?"

We both laughed and said, "Not me!"

As we stood in line together, the other girl who had been pushing and shoving overheard what I'd said about God seeing and hearing everything. She wanted to do the right thing. So she told Mr. Gab that she jumped in front of the girl with the long black hair and how sorry she was.

Mr. Gab then said to her, "Thank you for telling the truth."

At that moment, I realized you never know who's watching or listening to you.

It felt great to help. When Mr. Gab called the girl with the long black hair to the front of the line, she looked back at me and smiled.

Right before the bell rang, Mr. Gab gave a speech as he often does.

"I just want to say that I'm proud of each and every one of you. You'll become the light of the world, which can never be hidden. I know as you step into the future, you'll always remember to do the right thing. And if you choose the wrong path, I believe that you'll always listen to that little voice that says no and find your way back. I have faith in you and in your angels."

As I walked down the hall, I gripped my carnival tickets so tightly. I could taste that funnel cake. When we made it outside, I decided the food stand would be my first stop. There were seven people in line ahead of me. When it was my turn, I said in a high, squeaky voice, *"One funnel cake, please, and a lemonade!"*

I sat down at the closest table and watched my classmates ride the bumper cars.

I'll ride the bumper cars after I ride the mile-high swings. My funnel cake was hot with just the right amount of sugar sprinkled on it. After my second bite, I couldn't help but notice a girl wearing a ruffled shirt who had been staring at the lemonade stand for quite some time.

By the time I took my fourth bite, I wondered what she was doing so I asked, "Excuse me. Do you need some help?"

She responded by shaking her head no. "I want a corn dog, but I'm afraid my friends will call me fat. I'm not as skinny as them, and maybe I do eat too much. I shouldn't buy anything."

I thought to myself, *She's bigger than me,* and at that moment, I heard a whisper, "Don't be the ugly girl. *Ugly girls only see beauty in themselves. God made us all in his own image.*"

"Can I ask you a question?" I asked the girl wearing the ruffled shirt. "How do you think God sees you?"

She replied with a smile, "I think he loves my big brown eyes and my smile, but he's probably not too happy with my hands and maybe my legs. They're too big, but you should see my sister; she's perfect! She wears a size one, and I wear a six."

"Hey," I responded, "we wear the same size, and I believe God made me just the way I'm supposed to be, in his own image. I don't think one corn dog will hurt you. Now two or three, that's when we have to have self-control so that we can stay active and healthy. What does your sister think about you?"

"My sister says I'm beautiful and that she wishes she was my size. She thinks she's too skinny," she responded with a smile. "I guess we all have something we would change about ourselves, but if God made us in his own image, then we're all beautiful and should love ourselves. Thanks! I'll only eat one corn dog."

I laughed as the girl in the ruffled shirt bit into her corn dog and got mustard all over her fingers—and so did she.

As I finished my last bite of funnel cake and wiped the powdered sugar from my mouth, Mr. Gab stood in the food line. He ordered an extra-long corn dog, and after he paid for his food, he put his change in his back pocket. As he walked away, a dollar fell to the ground. Just as I was about to call out Mr. Gab's name, a girl wearing a blue skirt picked it up and smiled.

She had seen Mr. Gab drop it.

Her friend said, "You should keep it. Finders keepers, losers weepers."

I was hoping she would do the right thing. Well, it's only a dollar. Then the girl with the blue skirt said, "This isn't the first time I've found money. People drop it, and I pick it up. One day, this old lady dropped a twenty-dollar bill right in front of me. I waited for her to walk away, and I put it in my pocket. It's not my fault people lose things for me to find."

The girl in the blue skirt walked away laughing.

I thought to myself, If she lost something of value, then she would know how it feels. After I finished the best lemonade ever, I rushed over to the Ferris wheel.

The girl with the blue skirt and her friends were at the front of the line. There were too many people in front of me, so I had to wait until the next ride. Everyone was happy. Some of the students held their hands up as they went 'round and 'round. Many yelled, "Faster! Faster!" Then it was my turn. I was up so high that I tried to touch the closest cloud.

After the ride was over, I got back in line. I had to ride the Ferris wheel twice. When it was over, I thought, I should ride one last time, and just as I was about to get in line again, I saw the girl with the blue skirt and her friends searching for something. They were in a panic, asking everyone if they had found any money.

Everyone they asked answered no. The girl with the blue skirt started crying.

I thought to myself, *She deserved it. Now she knows how it feels to lose something.* At that moment, I heard a whisper.

"Don't be the ugly girl. *Ugly girls have no compassion. Understanding is what she needs.*"

Then at that moment, I felt sorry for her. I went over to her and said, "I'm sorry you lost your money. I saw you pick up Mr. Gab's dollar. Do you think someone waited for you to walk away and picked up your money when you dropped it?"

She replied, with a shaky voice, "Maybe. I know now how it feels to lose something. I should've given Mr. Gab his dollar when I saw him drop it. That wasn't right. Now I don't know what to do!"

Her friend said, "I bet if you wait a minute, you'll find more money." Then she laughed.

The girl with the blue skirt replied, "No, I'm going to do the right thing from this day forth. If I see someone drop something, I'm going to tell them, and you should too. I'm going to start right now. Excuse me, Mr. Gab? I have to tell you something."

After the girl with the blue skirt told Mr. Gab what had happened, he smiled and what he said next made her smile.

He said, "I was walking past the Ferris wheel, and a student getting off called out my name and said the seat she was sitting in had money in it and she knew someone was going to be looking for it. She wanted to do the right thing. Your money is in the office. Come; I'll take you there."

I've always heard the seeds you sow you reap, and now I know what that means. If you do good things, good things happen. If you do bad, bad things happen. I also know that nothing happens without God allowing it, but we should always do what's right no matter what. I was happy she was happy.

21

This is the best day ever!

As I was walking toward the mile-high swings, I heard a little girl yell, "No, I'm tired of doing what you say! We haven't ridden any of the rides I like, and that's not right!"

A girl wearing a pink hat responded with a yell, "If you don't do what I say, I'm not going to be your friend and I'm going to tell everyone not to play with you anymore!"

The little girl walked away, and when she saw another friend, standing by the bumper cars, she rushed over, smiled, and asked, "Hey, can you ride the mile-high swing with me?"

Then the girl with the pink hat rushed over and whispered to the girl the little girl was talking to, "Say no. I don't like her, and you shouldn't either. She's mean."

The girl in the pink hat told everyone not to play with the little girl or talk to her.

I thought to myself, *The little girl should tell everyone not to play with the girl in the pink hat first. Then she wouldn't be standing alone or sad.* And at that moment, I heard a whisper.

"Don't be the ugly girl. *Ugly girls are selfish. Two wrongs are never right.*"

I walked over to the little girl sitting on the bench, crying, and said, "Hi! I'm Faith. I need someone to ride the mile-high swings with me."

The little girl looked at me, smiled, and said with excitement, "Yes, I will!"

Just as we were getting in line, the girl with the pink hat rushed over to us with two of her friends and said, "If I were you, I wouldn't play with her; she's mean."

I responded, "She's not mean to me. She's my friend. Why are you being so mean to her?"

The little girl yelled out, "She's always mean to me. She does it when I won't do what she says, and Mom tells her to stop, but she doesn't listen."

The girl in the pink hat yelled as she stared at the little girl, "That's because I'm the oldest and Dad says she has to listen to me, no matter what."

"A real friend or sister," responded the little girl, "would never treat anyone like you do. Faith is my friend, and I'm going to ride the swings with her."

The brave little girl then turned toward the two girls who were standing with her sister and said, "And I don't know why you two are friends with her. She's always mean to you too, making you do things you don't want to and yelling all the time."

The tallest girl turned toward the girl wearing the pink hat and said, "Your sister is right. I remember when you told everyone not to play with me at lunchtime all because I wouldn't let you have my cupcake. I don't want to be your friend anymore."

The two girls walked away, and the girl wearing the pink hat was all alone.

As the little girl and I stood in the mile-high swing line, we couldn't help but notice the girl wearing the pink hat, sitting on the bench crying.

I whispered to the little girl, "I think she's learned her lesson, and I think she'll be a much better sister now!"

She responded, "I think so too, and if it's okay with you, I'd like to ask her to ride the swings with us."

"Sure," I replied. "I think that would make God smile. But wait! There're only two seats. You two should ride together, and I'll be right behind you."

The girl wearing the pink hat gave her sister the biggest hug, and they rode every ride together. The two sisters and I went our separate ways, and I couldn't help but smile as I watched them rush over to ride the bumper cars while holding hands.

After I rode the swings twice, I ran over to the hot-air balloons.

Wow, that's high, almost to the clouds!

They flew over a hundred feet in the sky.

I was running so fast, looking up, and I wasn't watching were I was going. I couldn't take my eyes off the balloon. I bumped into a tall girl and almost knocked her down. I apologized, but she didn't accept my apology.

She shoved me and then pushed me down.

Mr. Mike yelled out, "That's enough! Are you okay, Faith?"

Before I could respond, the tall girl answered, "She's fine. She bumped into me and fell down. She apologized, and I accepted."

The tall girl lied, and that made her a *liar.* I told Mr. Mike I was okay, and I was.

After the tall girl and her friends walked away, I waited in line to ride the balloons.

As the balloon went up and up, my hair waved in the wind and my heart was beating so fast. When I tried to look down, my knees shook. Then, finally, I gained enough courage to take a glance. The people below looked like ants, and I could see my house.

I can truly say I was thrilled when we were on the ground. I'm not afraid of heights, but five minutes of flying in the sky was enough for me. When I heard the bell ring and the teachers saying, "Ten minutes to home time, everyone!" I knew I only had time to ride one more ride—and that would be the bumper cars.

As I stood in line waiting my turn, I felt someone lightly pull my hair. When I looked back, the tall girl and her friends were in line behind me. I thought maybe it was my imagination and no one had pulled my hair. I ran over to drive car number 7, but the attendant said it wasn't working.

He told me to try car number 1. As he checked my seat buckle to make sure it was secure, the tall girl pointed at me with a smirk. When the attendant yelled, "On the count of three, let's have fun!" I gripped the steering wheel tightly. I was ready.

"One, two, three, *go!*"

I bumped into one of my classmates, and we laughed, but what happened next wasn't funny.

The tall girl and her friends surrounded me and bumped my car on all sides continuously until they had bumped me into a corner. A girl with bangs yelled out, "Hit her!"

I couldn't get out of the corner, and it seemed they'd never stop. Then the attended yelled, "Time's up!"

They high-fived each other and laughed. I was very angry. I was being bullied. As I began to walk away, my knee started hurting. When I looked down, my leg was bleeding.

Then I heard Mr. Mike say, "It's time to go home, everyone. I'll see some of you next year."

As I limped to the restroom to wipe away the blood from the scrape on my leg, the thought of being bullied was scary, but I knew that bullies are only obstacles to conquer. I knew with God on my side, fear wasn't for me. I prayed for the right thing to do and for strength on the way home. As I walked out of the restroom, the tall girl was leaning on the lockers across from the water fountain.

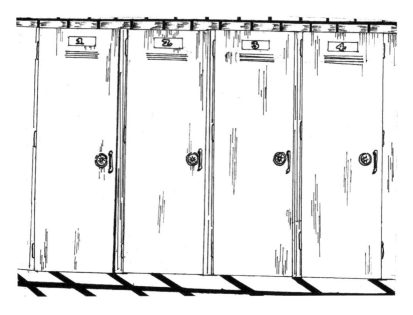

She looked at me, and I looked at her and stood tall. I wasn't going to be bullied any further.

God didn't give me a spirit of fear but of peace and of a sound mind. *I will conquer obstacles!*

She said, "You need to apologize for making me hurt my hand on the bumper cars."

Just as I was about to walk away, the tall girl's friend threw water in my face.

Then someone yelled out, "Fight!"

The tall girl tried to hit me, but I quickly moved and she slipped in the puddle of water.

The girl wearing the pink hat and her sister laughed, as did several others. I realized the tall girl had bullied many of them. *Yes, she was bigger in height and size, but she was slow at moving around. Every bully has a weakness, and I was going to prove to everyone how weak she was.*

Then, at that moment, I heard a whisper.

"Don't be the ugly girl. *Ugly girls are bullies. Don't stoop to her level. She doesn't know how to be a* godly friend, *but you do.*

When she stood to her feet, the back of her shorts were wet. The girl in a yellow shirt yelled, "What? You couldn't make it to the restroom? She needs a diaper."

31

Everyone laughed.

Then the tall girl said to her friend, "Hold her so I can hit her!"

But when her friend tried to grab me, the girl who had been sitting by the flagpole crying this morning, jumped in front of me and yelled, "No, let her fight her own battle. Let's see how tough she really is!"

When the tall girl tried to hit me again, I quickly ducked and she hit Mr. Mike in the arm.

Everyone froze, as did the tall girl when she realized she'd hit a teacher. Mr. Mike didn't flinch. He took a deep breath and said to her, "Follow me; this will be your last fight in my school!"

Mr. Gab then told me to follow Mr. Mike to the office. I wasn't afraid; I hadn't done anything wrong—or had I? *Was I the ugly girl?* As we sat in the office waiting for the principal, I turned toward the tall girl and asked, "Are you okay?"

She looked at me, smirked, and then quickly turned her head.

I then asked, "Do you like bullying people? Do you know what a godly friend is? That's someone who likes you for you, not because they're afraid of you! I never want to be friends with someone who tries to intimidate or belittle me. Just because you're taller than many of us and bigger, that doesn't mean everyone's afraid of you. Most times, bullies are being bullied, maybe at home or by a sister?"

The tall girl responded, "You don't know anything about me or my family, and I have friends! Oh yeah, and I'm still going to beat you up."

"You will lose," I responded. "In Jesus's name! I would love for you to see what kind of friend you could be if you truly wanted to be."

The principal called me into his office first. He only asked one question: "What would you like to see happen here?"

I responded, *"I would love for the tall girl's hurt or pain to go away, so that she can become a godly friend. Most bullies bully others because their hiding some type of insecurity and they're the ones that need the most love. I wonder why she called the girl sitting by the flagpole this morning, clothes ugly."*

The principal walked over toward me, touched me on my shoulder, and said, *"God loves to be revealed, I truly do!"*

When he touched me, it felt like electricity. When I walked past the tall girl, she wouldn't look at me. The principal called her into the office. He didn't say anything; he only touched her on the shoulder, and her eyes closed. They were only closed for a sminute. When she looked at me through the window, she looked different, like she was glowing.

"Just one touch from God," Mr. Mike said, "can change any heart!"

So it's true. Many have met angels and didn't know. That's why you should be kind to everyone. My work at Grace Jr. High was done, and now I understand why Mr. Gab—or should I say, *Gabriel*—was always there, guiding me with wisdom. He was my angel, and I was the tall girl's. *I could've wished for the tall girl to disappear but I prayed for her heart to change and from that day forth, the tall girl became a godly friend and I received my wings!*

Printed in the United States
By Bookmasters

R U THE UGLY BOY?

If You Teach Self-Worth through the Eyes of Christ
Jesus, Self-Esteem Will Come with Humility

TAKIA TEKE

Illustrated by

J. Sterling Jackson

WESTBOW
PRESS®
A DIVISION OF THOMAS NELSON
& ZONDERVAN

WestBow Press books may be ordered through booksellers or by contacting:

WestBow Press
A Division of Thomas Nelson & Zondervan
1663 Liberty Drive
Bloomington, IN 47403
www.westbowpress.com
1 (866) 928-1240

ISBN: 978-1-5127-6680-6 (sc)
ISBN: 978-1-5127-6681-3 (e)

Library of Congress Control Number: 2016919932

Print information available on the last page.

WestBow Press rev. date: 2/1/2017

Last Day of School!

Today was the best day of my life, and it started like all the others. God woke me up.

I brushed my teeth and thanked the Lord for another day.

This was the last day of school, the end-of-the-year carnival.

It seemed this day would never come. I was so excited.

Since today was super special, only the best outfit would do—and let's not forget shoes. When I looked in the mirror, I thought I was perfect!

Today, I would say, "Good-bye, Grace Jr. High, and Hello, Wisdom High School!"

carnival, carnival, carnival!

Ferris wheels,

funnel cakes, and

friends!

When I first arrived at school, there was a boy sitting on the steps next to the flagpole crying. He had his hands folded across his lap, and his head was down.

It was the strangest thing; I was the only one who noticed him. Everyone else—teacher, student, or parent—walked right past him. Even Mr. Gab did, and he noticed everyone—yes, everybody.

"Excuse me? My name is Wise. Are you all right?' I asked the boy who was crying.

He mumbled, "No, a tall boy called my clothes ugly and said my shoes didn't match. I searched my entire closet, and my dad helped me pick them out. Do you think my clothes are ugly?" He anxiously awaited my answer.

I looked at his clothes and then his shoes. I thought to myself, *I'd never wear that.*

And at that very moment, I heard a whisper.

"Don't be the ugly boy. *Ugly boys say mean things. We're all special in God's eyes, even in style.*"

I looked at him, smiled, and said, "I like what you're wearing because you like it. This would be a boring world if we all dressed alike. Clothes can only make the outside handsome, but when you say mean things, you look ugly on the inside and the out. That's why God looks at the heart."

He laughed. His laugh made me smile. As we stood to our feet, the bell rang and Mr. Gab called out my name. "Wise, come now; you don't want to be late."

I turned my head for a *sminute*—that's half of a minute—and the boy was gone.

I hope he has a wonderful last day of school.

As I walked down the hall, humming my happy song, I noticed everyone I passed was in a wonderful mood, but when I entered my classroom, everyone was laughing at the meanest boy in school.

He bent down to pick up his pencil and split his shorts right down the middle.

I wanted to laugh with the class, and maybe he deserved it. *He called me four eyes over a thousand times. He even hid my glasses, and when Mr. Gab found them on his desk under his hat, the lenses were missing.*

To make things worse, he told me he did it. And just as I was about to laugh, I heard a whisper.

"Don't be the ugly boy. *Ugly boys laugh when someone is hurting. What if you were in his shoes, what if he was you? He needs a friend."*

I then remembered he was nice to everyone until that cold day in November when he couldn't find his coat and had to ride the bus home in the cold.

I guess sometimes pain can make you mean, but kindness always helps you find friends. I gave him the extra pair of shorts that I had in my locker and said, "Sorry you tore your shorts."

He asked, "Why are you being nice to me?"

"That's what friends do," I responded. "It's never too late to make a friend!"

When I noticed Mr. Gab watching and smiling, it felt good to do something nice, but when the boy asked, "Wise, friends forever?" I felt *super* good inside. Like Mr. Gab always says, "A friend must first show himself friendly."

As I sat, anxiously awaiting the bell, I could see the Ferris wheel going 'round and 'round from the window.

I wanted to be the first to ride everything.

As Mr. Gab passed out the white envelopes filled with our carnival tickets, it felt like time was moving *oh so slowly*.

Was this a moment when patience was needed?

Was this a moment when good things would come to those who waited?

That's what my father always said.

But it couldn't be; I wasn't the only one excited.

When Mr. Gab passed the last envelope to the boy in the front row, I wondered where mine was.

"Wise," Mr. Gab asked, "are you sure you purchased tickets?"

"Yes," I responded. "Remember, we laughed when I was the first in line and it wasn't time? We were only going to math class."

"You're right," Mr. Gab responded. "I do remember. Okay, class, please make sure you have the right envelope. Wise's is missing. Check and see if there's two stuck together."

I felt a little mad so I raised my hand to go to the restroom, and as I walked down the hall, I said a prayer.

"Dear, Lord, it's Wise again. I need a moment of your time. I believe you can hear me and you see all things. I know you know where my envelope is. Can you please show me? Thank you, in Jesus's name. I do believe!"

As I walked back to class, I saw a boy wearing a black shirt, standing by my classroom. He was holding an envelope, and it had my name on it.

"My carnival tickets!" I screamed, using my inside voice. When the boy wearing the black shirt raised his head and saw my enormous smile, he didn't smile back. I couldn't believe what he did next. He placed my envelope behind his back and then walked to Mr. Mike's class.

I knew the right thing to do was to tell my teacher, but at that moment, *I was angry, very upset! I followed him, and I thought, I should snatch my envelope right out of his hand. It's mine!* Then at that moment, I heard a whisper.

"Don't be the ugly boy. *Ugly boys take things that don't belong to them. Ugly boys steal. The truth always shines through when you do what's right.*"

I thought to myself, Whether it is or isn't my envelope, the right thing to do is to tell my teacher. What if I'm wrong and it's not my envelope?

Mr. Mike, Mr. Gab, the boy in the black shirt, and I met in the hallway outside of Mr. Mike's class.

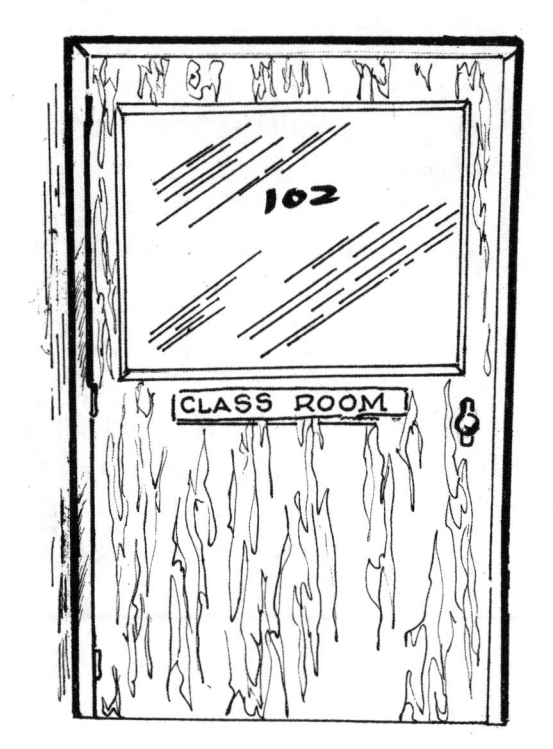

The boy in the black shirt apologized as he gave me my envelope.

He said, "I'm sorry, Wise, I took your carnival tickets. My parents didn't have the money to buy me any, and I know that's not a good reason to take what doesn't belong to me. Please forgive me?"

As I looked into his eyes, I thought, Everyone has to ask for forgiveness once or twice in their life. I know it's not right to take things that are not ours, but if God can forgive me when I'm wrong or mean to someone, then I can forgive him. I responded, "I forgive you, and if it's okay with Mr. Gab and Mr. Mike, I'd like to share my tickets with you. I have more than enough."

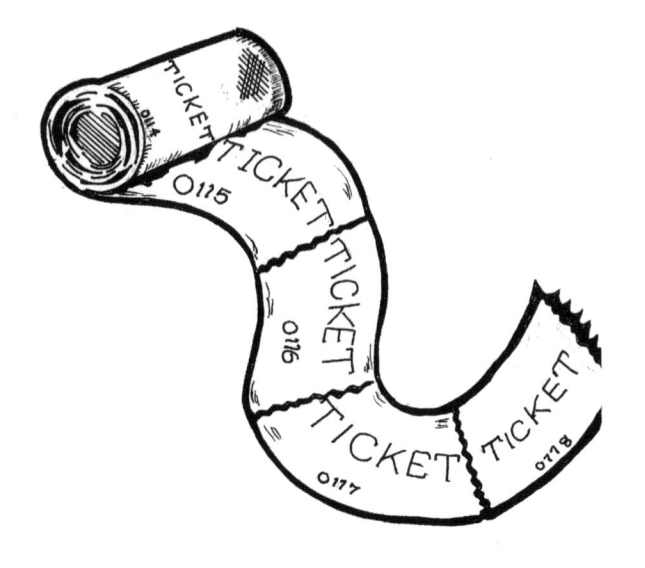

The boy in the black shirt smiled as our teachers both replied, "Sure, that's fine."

I felt good inside!

As we entered the class, the bell rang and all the children started screaming, "It's noon! It's carnival time!" As we lined up one last time, two students started pushing, shoving, and yelling at one another.

"I was here first!"

"No, I was!"

"Move!"

"I'm going to tell!"

Mr. Gab shouted, "Enough! You both go to the back of the line."

As both boys sadly walked past me, one boy with short red hair looked at me with the meanest look and asked, "What are you looking at?"

And then he called me a *bad name*.

Mr. Gab didn't hear him, and I couldn't believe he had said that. I knew words didn't hurt, *but I wanted to call him a name just as mean as the one he had called me.* At that moment, I heard a whisper.

"Don't be the ugly boy. *Ugly boys say bad words. Kind words make God smile. Love and kindness can make all boys handsome. God hears us, even our whispers.*"

So I said to the boy with the short red hair, "I'm sorry you're angry, but I didn't do it and I didn't deserve to be called a bad name. No one does. So I think you owe me an apology. If you wouldn't say that word in front of your parents, then don't say it in front of God or to me. God hears and sees everything, right and wrong."

He said, "I'm sorry. You're right; my dad would be extremely mad if he heard me say that word to you. I'm sorry!"

"If God can forgive me, then I can forgive you," I responded. "We're too handsome to say bad words. We should never speak to one another with cursing jests. Bad words make you look ugly. And who wants to be ugly like a monster?"

We both laughed and said, "Not me!"

As we stood in line together, the other boy who had been pushing and shoving overheard what I'd said about God seeing and hearing everything. He wanted to do the right thing. So he told Mr. Gab that he did jump in front of the boy with the short red hair and how sorry he was.

Mr. Gab then said to him, "Thank you for telling the truth."

At that moment, I realized you never know who's watching or listening to you.

It felt great to help. When Mr. Gab called the boy with the short red hair to the front of the line, he looked back at me and smiled.

Right before the bell rang, Mr. Gab gave a speech as he often does.

"I just want to say that I'm proud of each and every one of you. You'll become the light of the world, which can never be hidden. I know as you step into the future, you'll always remember to do the right thing. And if you choose the wrong path, I believe that you'll listen to that little voice that says *no* and find your way back. I have faith in you and in your angels."

As I walked down the hall, I gripped my carnival tickets tightly. I could taste that funnel cake. When we made it outside, I decided the food stand would be my first stop. There were seven people in line ahead of me. When it was my turn, I said in a high, squeaky voice, *"One funnel cake, please, and a lemonade!"*

I sat down at the closest table and watched my classmates ride the bumper cars.

I'll ride the bumper cars after I ride the mile-high swings. My funnel cake was hot with just the right amount of sugar sprinkled on it. After my second bite, I couldn't help but notice a boy who had been standing and staring at the lemonade stand for quite some time. By the time I took my fourth bite, I wondered what he was doing, so I asked, "Excuse me. Do you need some help?"

He responded by shaking his head no. "I want a corn dog, but I'm afraid my friends will call me fat. I'm not as skinny as them, and maybe I do eat too much. I shouldn't buy anything."

I thought to myself, *He's bigger than me,* and at that moment, I heard a whisper.

"Don't be the ugly boy. *Ugly boys only see greatness in themselves. God made us all in his own image.*"

"Can I ask you a question?" I asked the boy staring at the lemonade stand. "How do you think God sees you?"

He replied with a laugh, "I think he loves that I'm thoughtful and my smile, but he's probably not too happy with my stomach and maybe my legs. They're too big, but you should see my brother; he's all muscle. I wear a size sixteen in pants."

"Hey," I responded, "we wear the same size and I believe God made me just the way I'm supposed to be, in his own image. I don't think one corn dog will hurt you. Now, two or three, that's when we have to have self-control so that we can stay active and healthy. What does your brother think about you?"

"My brother says I'm fit and he wishes he was my size. He thinks he's too skinny," he responded with a laugh. "I guess we all have something we would change about ourselves, but if God made us in his own image, then we're all handsome and should love ourselves. Thanks! I'll only eat one corn dog."

I laughed as the boy bit into his corn dog and got mustard all over his shirt—and so did he.

As I finished my last bite of funnel cake and wiped the powdered sugar from my mouth, Mr. Gab stood in the food line. He ordered an extra-long corn dog, and after he paid for his food, he put his change in his back pocket. As he walked away, a dollar fell to the ground, and just as I was about to call out Mr. Gab's name, a boy wearing blue jeans picked it up and smiled.

He had seen Mr. Gab drop it.

His friend said, "You should keep it. Finders keepers, losers weepers."

I was hoping he would do the right thing. *Well, it's only a dollar.*

Then the boy wearing the blue jeans said, "This isn't the first time I've found money. People drop it, and I pick it up. One day, this old man dropped a twenty-dollar bill right in front of me. I waited for him to walk away, and I put it in my pocket. It's not my fault people lose things for me to find."

The boy in the blue jeans walked away, laughing.

I thought to myself, If he lost something of value, then he would know how it feels. After I finished the best lemonade ever, I rushed over to the Ferris wheel.

The boy wearing blue jeans and his friends were in the front of the line. There were too many people in front of me, so I had to wait until the next ride. Everyone was happy. Some of the students held their hands up as they went 'round and 'round. Many yelled, "Faster! Faster!" Then it was my turn. I was up so high that I tried to touch the closest cloud. After the ride was over, I got back in line. I had to ride the Ferris wheel twice. When it was over, I thought, I should ride one last time, and just as I was about to get in line again, I saw the boy wearing the blue jeans and his friends searching for something. They were in a panic, asking everyone if they had found any money.

Everyone they asked answered no. The boy wearing the blue jeans started crying.

17

I thought, He deserved it. *Now he knows how it feels to lose something*, and at that moment, I heard a whisper.

"Don't be the ugly boy. *Ugly boys have no compassion. Understanding is what he needs."*

Then, at that moment, I felt sorry for him. I went over to him and said, "I'm sorry you lost your money. I saw you pick up Mr. Gab's dollar. Do you think someone waited for you to walk away and picked up your money when you dropped it?"

He replied with a shaky voice, "Maybe. I know now how it feels to lose something. I should've given Mr. Gab his dollar when I saw him drop it. That wasn't right. Now I don't know what to do!"

His friend said, "I bet if you wait a minute, you'll find more money." Then he laughed.

The boy wearing blue jeans replied, "No, I'm going to do the right thing from this day forth. If I see someone drop something, I'm going to tell them and you should too. I'm going to start right now. Excuse me, Mr. Gab. I have to tell you something."

After the boy wearing blue jeans told Mr. Gab what had happened, he smiled, and what Mr. Gab said next made him smile too.

He said, "I was walking past the Ferris wheel, and a student getting off called out my name and said the seat he was sitting in had money in it and he knew someone was going to be looking for it. He wanted to do the right thing. Your money is in the office. Come; I'll take you there."

I've always heard the seeds you sow you reap, and now I know

what that means. If you do good things, good things happen. If you do bad, bad things happen. I also know that nothing happens without God allowing it, but we should always do what's right, no matter what. I was happy he was happy.

This is the best day ever!

As I was walking toward the mile-high swings, I heard a little boy yell, "No, I'm tired of doing what you say. We haven't ridden any of the rides I like, and that's not right!"

A boy wearing a green hat responded with a yell, "If you don't do what I say, I'm not going to be your friend and I'm going to tell everyone not to play with you anymore!"

The little boy walked away, and when he saw another friend standing by the bumper cars, he rushed over, smiled, and asked, "Hey, can you ride the mile-high swings with me?"

Then the boy with the green hat rushed over and whispered to the boy the little boy was talking to, "Say no. I don't like him, and you shouldn't either. He's mean."

The boy in the green hat told everyone not to play with the little boy or talk to him.

I thought, *The little boy should tell everyone not to play with the boy in the green hat first. Then he wouldn't be standing alone or sad.* And at that moment, I heard a whisper.

"Don't be the ugly boy. *Ugly boys are selfish. Two wrongs are never right.*"

I walked over to the little boy sitting on the bench, crying, and said, "Hi, I'm Wise. I need someone to ride the mile-high swings with me."

The little boy looked at me, smiled, and said with excitement, "Yes, I will!"

Just as we were getting in line, the boy with the green hat rushed over toward us with two of his friends and said, "If I were you, I wouldn't play with him; he's mean."

I responded, "He's not mean to me. He's my friend. Why are you being so mean to him?"

The little boy yelled out, "He's always mean to me. He does it when I won't do what he says, and Dad tells him to stop, but he doesn't listen."

The boy in the green hat yelled as he glared at the little boy,

"That's because I'm the oldest and Mom says he has to listen to me no matter what."

"A real friend or brother," responded the little boy, "would never treat anyone like you do. Wise is my friend, and I'm going to ride the swings with him."

The brave little boy then turned toward the two boys who were standing with his brother and said, "And I don't know why you two are friends with him; he's always mean to you, making you do things you don't want to and yelling all the time."

The tallest boy turned toward the boy wearing the green hat and said, "Your brother is right. I remember when you told everyone not to play with me at lunchtime all because I wouldn't let you have my cupcake. I don't want to be your friend anymore."

The two boys walked away, and the boy wearing the green hat was all alone.

As the little boy and I stood in the mile-high swing line, we couldn't help but notice the boy wearing the green hat sitting on the bench and crying.

I whispered to the little boy, "I think he's learned his lesson and he'll be a much better brother now!"

He responded, "I think so too, and if it's okay with you, I'd like to ask him to ride the swings with us."

"Sure," I replied. "I think that would make God smile. But wait! There're only two seats. You two should ride together, and I'll be right behind you."

The boy wearing the green hat gave his brother the biggest hug, and they rode every ride together. The two brothers and I went our separate ways, and I couldn't help but smile as I watched them rush over to ride the bumper cars.

After I rode the swings twice, I ran over to the hot-air balloons.

Wow, that's high, almost to the clouds!

They flew over a hundred feet in the sky.

I was running so fast, looking up, and I wasn't watching were I was going. I couldn't take my eyes off the balloon. I bumped into a tall boy and almost knocked him down. I apologized, but he didn't accept my apology. He pushed me down.

Mr. Mike yelled out, "That's enough! Are you okay, Wise?"

Before I could respond, the tall boy answered, "He's fine. He bumped into me and fell down. He apologized, and I accepted."

The tall boy lied, and that made him a *liar.* I told Mr. Mike I was okay, and I was.

After the tall boy and his friends walked away, I waited in line to ride the balloons.

As the balloon went up and up, my hair waved in the wind and my heart was beating so fast. When I tried to look down, my knees shook. Then, finally, I gained enough courage to take a glance. All the people below looked like ants, and I could see my house.

I can truly say I was thrilled when we were on the ground. I'm not afraid of heights, but five minutes of flying in the sky was enough for me. When I heard the bell ring and the teachers say, "Ten minutes to home time, everyone," I knew I only had time to ride one more ride and that was the bumper cars.

As I stood in line, waiting my turn, I felt someone pull my shirt. When I looked back, I saw the tall boy and his friends were in line behind me. I thought maybe it was my imagination and no one had pulled my shirt. I ran over to drive car number 7, but the attendant said it wasn't working.

He told me to try car number 1. As he checked my seat buckle to make sure it was secure, the tall boy pointed at me with a smirk. When the attendant yelled, "On the count of three, let's have fun!" I gripped the steering wheel tightly. I was ready. "One, two, three, go!"

I bumped into one of my classmates, and we laughed, but what happened next wasn't funny.

The tall boy and his friends surrounded me and bumped my car on all sides continuously until they had bumped me into a corner. A boy with a scar on his face yelled out, "Hit him!" I couldn't get out of the corner, and it seemed they'd never stop.

Then the attendant yelled, "Time's up!"

They high-fived each other and laughed. I was very angry. I was being bullied. As I began to walk away, my knee started hurting. When I looked down, my leg was bleeding.

Then I heard Mr. Mike say, "It's time to go home, everyone. I'll see some of you next year."

I walked to the restroom to wiped the blood from the scrape on my leg, the thought of being bullied was scary, but I knew that bullies were only obstacles to conquer. I knew with God on my side, fear wasn't for me. I prayed for the right thing to do and for strength on the way home. When I walked out of the restroom, the tall boy was leaning on the lockers across from the water fountain.

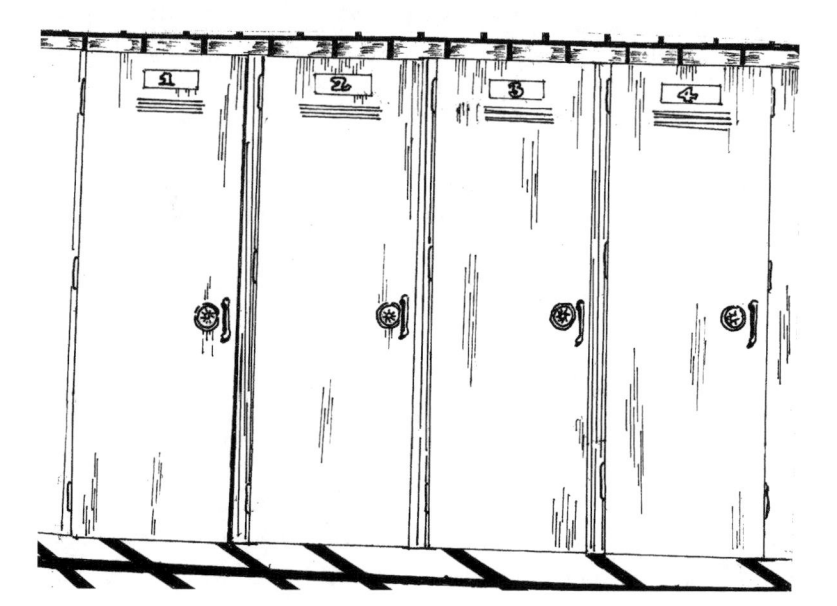

He looked at me, and I looked at him and stood tall. I wasn't going to be bullied any further.

God didn't give me a spirit of fear but of peace and of a sound mind. I will conquer obstacles!

He said, "You need to apologize for making me hurt my hand on the bumper cars."

Just as I was about to walk away, the tall boy's friend threw water in my face.

Then someone yelled out, "Fight!"

The tall boy tried to hit me, but I quickly moved and he slipped in the puddle of water. The boy wearing the green hat and his brother laughed, as did several others. I realized the tall boy had bullied many of them. *Yes, he was bigger in height and size, but*

he was slow at moving around. Every bully has a weakness, and I was going to prove to everyone how weak he was. I rubbed my hands together and smiled.

Then, at that moment, I heard a whisper.

"Don't be the ugly boy. *Ugly boys are bullies. Don't stoop to his level. He doesn't know how to be a* godly friend, *but you do.*"

When he stood to his feet, the back of his shorts were wet.

The boy wearing the black shirt yelled, "What? You couldn't make it to the restroom?"

Everyone laughed.

Then the tall boy said to his friend, "Hold him so I can hit him!"

But when his friend tried to grab me, the boy who had been sitting by the flagpole crying this morning jumped in front of me and yelled, "No, let him fight his own battle. Let's see how tough he really is! Oh and my clothes are not ugly, right Wise?"

When the tall boy tried to hit me again, I quickly ducked and he hit Mr. Mike in the arm.

Everyone froze, as did the tall boy when he realized he'd hit a teacher. Mr. Mike didn't flinch. He took a deep breath and said to him, "Follow me. This will be your last fight in my school!"

Mr. Gab then told me to follow Mr. Mike to the office. I wasn't afraid. I hadn't done anything wrong—or had I? Was *I* the ugly

boy? As we sat in the office, waiting for the principal, I turned toward the tall boy and asked, "Are you okay?"

He looked at me, smiled, and then quickly turned his head.

I then asked, "Do you like bullying people? Do you know what a godly friend is? That's someone who likes you for you, not because they're afraid of you! I never want to be friends with someone who tries to intimidate or belittle me. Just because you're taller than many of us and bigger, that doesn't mean everyone's afraid of you. Most times, bullies are being bullied, maybe at home or by a brother?"

The tall boy responded quickly, "You don't know anything about me or my family, and I have friends! Oh yeah and I'm still going to beat you up."

"You will lose," I replied. "In Jesus's name! I would love for you to see what kind of friend you could be if you truly wanted to."

The principal called me into his office first. He only asked one question, *"What would you like to see happen to him?"*

I responded, "I would love for the tall boy's hurt and pain to go away. So that he can become a godly friend. The meanest people are the ones who need the most love."

The principal walked over toward me, touched me on my shoulder, and said, *"God loves to be revealed, I truly do!"*

When he touched me, it felt like electricity. When I walked past the tall boy, he wouldn't look at me. The principal called him into the office. He didn't say a word; he just touched him on the shoulder, and his eyes closed. They were only closed for a sminute. When he looked at me through the window, he looked different, like he was glowing.

"Just one touch from God," Mr. Mike said, "can change any heart, but it starts with yours!"

So it's true. Many have met angels and didn't know. That's why you should be kind to everyone. My work at Grace Jr. High was done, and now I understand why Mr. Gab—or should I say,

Gabriel—was always there guiding me with wisdom. He was my angel, and I was the tall boy's. *I could've wished for the tall boy to go away, but I prayed for his heart to change, and from that day forth, the tall boy became a godly friend and I received my wings!*

Takia Teke is the founder of One Flesh Ministry, wife and mother of three. She wrote her first novel in the ninth grade. She's performed her collection of poetry all over the Midwest. She credits her mother Carol and grandmother Ruth for her love of writing and performing. She surrendered her life to Christ Jesus in 2006 and has no desire to return to Egypt. She's written seven novels, six screenplays and over thirty children books. Her children are her inspiration behind this title. She wants them to become Godly Friends and to understand when someone isn't. Takia Teke is a 2015 MICAH award winner with United Congregations of Metro East and one of the youngest Poets published in the magazine, DRUMVOICES REVIEW. She says, "When God makes you a promise it's written in stone."